For the Right to Learn
Malala Yousafzai's Story

by Rebecca Langston-George

illustrated by Janna Bock

Content Consultant: Yasmin Saikia
Professor of History and Hardt-Nickachos Chair in Peace Studies
Arizona State University

CAPSTONE PRESS
a capstone imprint

Scarcely 5 feet tall and only 17 years old, a schoolgirl from Pakistan stood before the microphone. Her courage was legendary. World leaders leaned forward to listen. As Malala Yousafzai accepted the Nobel Peace Prize in Oslo, Norway, cameras carried her message around the world.

In her home country, a female could be beaten for public speaking. But Malala was not afraid. Strength, power, and courage pulsed inside her. She became the youngest Nobel Peace Prize winner on December 10, 2014. Malala lifted her voice for children everywhere.

"This award is not just for me. It is for those forgotten children who want education. It is for those frightened children who want peace. It is for those voiceless children who want change."

Malala had become the voice for equal education. She almost lost her life for it.

Malala's own education started early. Her father, Ziauddin Yousafzai, ran a school in Mingora, a town surrounded by snowcapped mountains in the Swat Valley of Pakistan. From the time she could walk she visited classes. She even pretended to teach. Malala loved school.

Not all Pakistani children had Malala's opportunities. Many families couldn't afford to pay for school. Others only paid for their sons' educations. Those parents believed daughters should cook and keep house.

Malala's own mother didn't learn to read or write when she was young. But Malala's father believed girls deserved the same education as boys. He encouraged Malala and her younger brothers, Khushal and Atal, to study. He also let many poor children attend his school for free.

Malala thrived at school. She worked hard and received many trophies and awards. Not only could she speak and write her native Pashto language, but she also spoke fluent English and Urdu, Pakistan's national language.

But Taliban leaders who controlled the area were against letting girls go to school. They declared that females should be separated from males. They wanted to outlaw education for girls. They also tried to force women to wear garments called burqas to cover their entire bodies and faces.

Members of the Taliban intimidated school leaders. One ordered Ziauddin to close his school because girls and boys used the same entrance. When Malala's father refused, the Taliban threatened the teachers until some of them quit.

Ziauddin grew worried. But Malala wasn't. "The girls of Swat aren't afraid of anyone." She was more determined than ever to succeed at school. Over the school holidays most Pakistani women used henna to paint flowers and vines on their hands. Malala covered her hands with science formulas.

The Taliban grew stronger every day through violence and intimidation. As their strength grew, so did the rules. Men could not shave. Women had to cover their faces. Movies were banned. Radios throughout the Swat Valley crackled with the sound of the Taliban preaching.

NO EDUCATION FOR GIRLS!
GIRLS WHO ATTEND SCHOOL
BRING SHAME TO THEIR FAMILIES!

Fear spread through Malala's homeland. Classrooms that were once full now had many empty seats. Taliban leaders bragged on the radio about those they had coerced. "We congratulate Aadab Tareen who has stopped going to school."

Ziauddin fought back, appearing on TV to stress the importance of education. Malala came with him. When a reporter asked for her opinion, she said, "How dare the Taliban take away my basic right to education!"

Later they found a letter taped to the school gate. "… The school you are running is Western … You teach girls … Stop this or you will be in trouble …"

Threats did not frighten Malala. She and her father kept demanding equal education for girls. They spoke to clubs, wrote letters to newspapers, and called journalists. Malala warned, "If this new generation is not given pens, they will be given guns by the terrorists."

But the situation grew worse. Members of the Taliban began patrolling the streets with machine guns. They beat people who broke curfew. Bombs exploded in the night. Businesses that didn't follow Taliban rules were heaps of rubble by morning.

Then, in December 2008, came the terrible radio announcement. "All girls' schools will close. Starting January 15th no girls will be allowed at school." Even before the deadline, bombs started to rain down on nearby schools as warnings.

But bombs could not silence Malala. The British Broadcasting Corporation (BBC) wanted a girl to blog about the school closings. The girl blogger would tell firsthand how it felt to be denied an education. Fearing jail, beatings, and even bombs, all her friends refused. Malala volunteered.

She borrowed her pen name, Gul Makai, from a Pakistani figure who had fought against British oppression long ago. Internet service and power were unreliable in Pakistan. So Gul Makai spoke by phone to a BBC reporter who typed her blog for the next two months. The blog first appeared in Urdu on January 3, 2009. Soon Malala's blog became popular, and the BBC translated it into English.

On January 14, 2009, she blogged, "I am of the view that the school will one day reopen, but while leaving I looked at the building as if I would not come here again." Malala was sad but defiant. "They can stop us going to school, but they can't stop us learning!"

Activists like Malala grew more and more angry. Finally, the Taliban began to allow girls who were 10 years old and younger to go to school. But Malala was 11. She and her friends left their blue school uniforms at home. Dressed in street clothes, they hid books under their shawls and pretended to be younger than they were. Lying about their ages was gravely dangerous. If caught, the students and their teacher would have been publicly beaten or executed.

Life grew more dangerous every day. Pakistan's army began to fight the Taliban. Gunfire and screams filled the air. No one, not even defiant schoolgirls, dared to brave the streets. In May 2009 the army announced everyone must evacuate. Cars, motorcycles, trucks, and donkey carts piled with possessions jammed the one open road. Taliban members watched from behind their machine guns as 2 million people fled the Swat Valley.

Hot tears trickled down Malala's face as she stuffed a few clothes into a small bag. She reached for her books, but her mother said there was no room. Heartbroken to leave them behind, Malala prayed her books would be there when she returned. Scrambling to get out with their lives, Malala's mother, father, and brothers crowded into a neighbor's van. Malala squeezed into her friend's car. The Taliban had already tried to take her rights, her education, and her voice. Malala prayed they wouldn't come after her home.

Refugees flooded the villages outside Swat Valley. The United Nations Refugee Committee opened camps filled with white tents to house people, but they quickly became overcrowded. Poor sanitation led to the spread of disease. Rumors of the Taliban infiltrating the camps sparked fear in many weary hearts. The Yousafzai family was fortunate to have relatives they could stay with. But the friends who had driven them out of Mingora were going elsewhere. With no car of their own, they walked the 16 hot, dusty miles.

Malala's 12th birthday came in July, but there was no celebration. No cake. No party. In fact, no one even remembered. But Malala made a birthday wish anyway. She wished for peace.

When they returned home three months later, the fighting had ended. But Mingora had changed. Shops were demolished. Gray skeletons of burned cars littered the roads. The school's walls were peppered with bullet holes. But there was no sign of the Taliban. Ziauddin resumed classes within days. Classes for boys and classes for girls!

Malala was back at school, but her life would never be the same. The Taliban's effort to ban girls from school had made international headlines. Friends and neighbors had guessed she was Gul Makai. Her blog, speeches, and interviews had made Malala internationally famous. South African Archbishop Desmond Tutu nominated her for an award. Pakistan renamed its peace prize to the National Malala Peace Prize in her honor. By the end of 2011, Malala's life was full of TV, radio, and newspaper interviews. Her picture was everywhere.

Soon Malala learned that the Taliban was not gone. Taliban leaders began to threaten her on the Internet. Saying she was working for the West, they announced Malala was on their hit list. The police warned the Yousafzai family to leave.

But Malala refused to hide.
She refused to be silenced.

Malala's mother, Tor Pekai, feared for her daughter's safety. Though the school was a short distance from their home, Tor Pekai insisted Malala ride the school bus. Despite her fears, she was proud of her daughter. In fact, Malala inspired her mother to go to school. Tor Pekai scheduled her first reading lesson for October 9, 2012.

As Tor Pekai arrived at school for her first lesson, Malala and her friends boarded the school bus to go home. Sitting on benches under the canvas roof, they laughed and sang. Suddenly the bus lurched to a stop. A man lifted the canvas cover.

"WHO IS MALALA?"

No one spoke. The only movement was the
girls' eyes darting in concern toward their friend.
That was enough. The man pointed a gun at Malala.

Three shots shattered the silence.

The bus driver sped Malala, along with her wounded friends Shazia and Kainat, to the hospital. Hours passed in a swirl of confusion. As word spread through the streets, journalists packed the hospital to cover the story. Ziauddin's phone rang as he gave a speech to other school leaders. He hurried to the hospital, pleading to the crowd, "Pray for Malala."

Tor Pekai arrived home as neighbors poured into the house with the bad news. A friend called to say Malala would be taken to another hospital by helicopter. Tor Pekai and her neighbors rushed to the roof to watch Malala's helicopter fly overhead. Lifting her head scarf into the wind, she prayed, "God, I entrust her to you."

Hours stretched into days, but Malala scarcely noticed. Her brain swelled. As she lay unconscious, the Taliban announced the girl would "not be spared," and she would be targeted again if she survived.

Doctors performed surgery to reduce the swelling in her brain. Then an infection nearly killed her. Eventually Malala was flown to a hospital in Birmingham, England, to receive more surgery and keep her safe from further attacks.

News of the girl shot by the Taliban spread around the world. As the girl who had fought for education fought for her life, thousands of cards arrived for her. Hundreds of stuffed animals and flowers poured into the hospital. But what Malala wanted most were her schoolbooks.

Doctors performed many surgeries on Malala over the next few months. Surgeons repaired her drooping eye and fixed her facial nerves so she could smile. They implanted a hearing device in her ear. She stayed in the hospital for three months. During that time her school friends in Mingora kept a seat empty for her.

Bullets did not silence Malala for long. On July 12, 2013, she delivered a speech before world leaders at the United Nations. She declared, "One child, one teacher, one book, and one pen can change the world." The audience responded with a standing ovation for the girl who had fought for the right to learn.

More About Malala's Story

Malala's home in the Swat Valley lies in the northern part of Pakistan. Close to Afghanistan, it shares cultural and historic ties with its Afghan neighbors. After terrorists attacked the United States on September 11, 2001, the United States and its allies sent troops to Afghanistan. The Taliban had grown very strong in that region, and many members of the Taliban moved to the Swat Valley during the military occupation. There the Taliban forced their ideas on the Pakistani people.

The bullet that struck Malala entered above her left eye socket, traveled down her face, and ended up in her shoulder. At first doctors believed she was not badly injured, but later they determined her injuries were life threatening. Her brain, facial nerves, and hearing were all damaged. To relieve the swelling on her brain, doctors removed part of her skull. They later replaced the removed skull bone with a metal plate. Her friends Shazia and Kainat suffered minor injuries.

The Birmingham, England, hospital could scarcely keep up with the thousands of cards and gifts that arrived for Malala. She treasured one gift in particular.

The late Benazir Bhutto's children sent two of their mother's shawls. Bhutto had been Pakistan's prime minister until she was assassinated. Malala counted Bhutto among her personal heroes. She proudly wore Bhutto's white shawl when speaking before the United Nations.

Almost two years after the shooting, the Pakistani Army arrested a group of 10 men who were involved in Malala's shooting. But the Taliban continue to issue threats against her.

Malala returned to school several months after the shooting. But because of the continuing threats, she couldn't go back to the seat she once filled in Mingora. She and her family now live in Birmingham. She will continue her education there so she can one day return to Pakistan armed not with guns, but with knowledge. She and her father continue to speak about education. Malala also started an organization to fund education in countries like Pakistan. She promises to continue to work toward "peace in every home" and "education for every boy and every girl in the world."

Glossary

ban (BAN)—to forbid something

coerce (koh-URSS)—to force someone to do something

henna (HEN-uh)—a reddish-brown dye

infiltrate (IN-fil-trate)—to secretly enter in order to spy or cause damage

intimidate (in-TIM-uh-date)—to threaten in order to force certain behavior

pen name (PEN NAME)—a name used by a writer instead of the writer's real name

prime minister (PRIME MIN-uh-stur)—in many nations, the head of government

refugee (ref-yuh-JEE)—a person forced to flee his or her home because of natural disaster or war

Taliban (TAL-i-ban)—a radical group that was controlling much of Afghanistan in the 1990s and early 2000s; the U.S. military and its allies helped remove the Taliban from power in 2001

United Nations (yoo-NI-ted NAY-shuns)—a group of countries that works together for peace and security

Index

Editor: Jennifer Besel
Designer: Lori Bye
Production Specialist: Tori Abraham
Creative Director: Nathan Gassman
The illustrations in this book were created digitally.

Encounter is published by Capstone,
1710 Roe Crest Drive, North Mankato, Minnesota 56003
www.capstonepub.com

Library of Congress Cataloging-in-Publication Data
Langston-George, Rebecca.
For the right to learn : Malala Yousafzai's story / by Rebecca Langston-George ; illustrated by Janna Bock.
pages cm. — (Encounter)
Includes bibliographical references and index.
Summary: "Tells Malala Yousafzai's harrowing story of standing up for girls' education against the Taliban, being shot in the head, and surviving to continue the fight"—Provided by publisher.
ISBN 978-1-4914-6071-9 (library binding) — ISBN 978-1-62370-426-1 (paper over board) — ISBN 978-1-4914-6556-1 (paperback) — ISBN 978-1-4914-6557-8 (ebook pdf)
1. Yousafzai, Malala, 1997—Juvenile literature 2. Young women—Education—Pakistan—Biography—Juvenile literature. 3. Children's rights—Pakistan—Juvenile literature. I. Bock, Janna, ill. II. Title.
LC2330.L35 2016
371.822095491—dc23
                                        2014041434

Direct quotations are found on the following pages:

p2: Nobel Lecture by Malala Yousafzai, Oslo, December 10, 2014; p11: "Malala Yousafzai's November 2011 speech on education," online by *Guardian News* http://www.theguardian.com/world/video/2012/oct/14/malala-yousafzai-speech-education-video; p15: *I Am Malala* by Malala Yousafzai and Christina Lamb (Little, Brown and Company: New York, 2013. p142, 121); p16: Mahr, Krista. "Malala Yousafzai: The Latest Victim in the War on Children in Pakistan," *Time*, October 9, 2012. http://world.time.com/2012/10/09/malala-yousafzai-the-latest-victim-in-pakistans-war-on-children/; p18: "Diary of a Pakistani schoolgirl," BBC http://news.bbc.co.uk/2/hi/south_asia/7834402.stm; *I Am Malala* (p161); p29: *I Am Malala* (p241); p32: *I Am Malala* (p247, 250); p35: "14-yr-old girl who took on Taliban in blog attacked," Rediff News, October 9, 2012. http://www.rediff.com/news/report/pak-14-yr-old-girl-who-took-on-taliban-in-blog-attacked/20121009.htm; p37: *I Am Malala* (p310); p38: *I Am Malala* (p313)

Image Credits:
Getty Images: Boston Globe, 39
Design elements: Shutterstock: blue67design, JungleOutThere, karakotsya

Printed and bound in the USA.
102018   000052